THE BLINDFOLD

Remove the Blindfold of Myths, Beliefs and thoughts that cover our mind

PRITTI M DHANUKKA

INDIA • SINGAPORE • MALAYSIA

ISBN 979-8-88986-998-6

THE BLINDFOLD

'Unravel the Blindfold of Myths, Beliefs, Biases and Thoughts to see the world and yourself in a new light'.

– PRITTI M DHANUKKA

Contents

Acknowledgement

I dedicate this book to my late Grandfather, Mr. Radheshyam Murarka, who laid the foundation of my character. Growing up I always felt like I was my Grandfather's Princess. But, he was also my first educator and tutor from whom I learned the great values of integrity, discipline and abundance. He used to wake me up at four o'clock in the morning right from the age of seven to teach me English and Maths. I am forever grateful for his influence on my life.

I also want to dedicate this book to my father-in-law, who only had the privilege of being a part of my life for five years after my marriage. However, those years were formative as he inspired me to work on my inner being, which has impacted my journey in significant ways.

I would like to dedicate this book to my mother, the late Mrs. Bina Devi Murarka, who had a timeless influence on my life. She was the epitome of resilience and willpower, fighting cancer for three years without any grudges. Even during her toughest times she remained positive and taught me the true meaning of strength and courage.

Although she is no longer with us, her memory continues to inspire me to strive for greatness in everything that I do. I am forever grateful for her unwavering love and guidance, and I know that her spirit will continue to live on with me through this book.

My husband has been my mirror for self-realization, and I owe a significant part of my self-empowerment journey to him. His healthy criticism and sharp observations have helped me evolve over the past twenty-four years of our togetherness.

I would also like to express my gratitude to my mentor, Arfeen Khan, who provided me with the system to transform my life. Last but not the least; I owe a special thanks to another mentor of mine—Irfaan Noorani, also known as the 'Clarity Man', without whom writing a book would have still been an unrealized dream.

Preface

Have you ever stopped to consider how your thinking patterns and perceptions might be holding you back?

In this book, I am going to demonstrate how we often think that external forces—our environment, society and relationships—are the source of our challenges. The actual truth is, when it comes to the quality of our life, we are the most important reason behind our successes and misfortunes.

Why am I talking about this?

When I was studying psychology in college, I was astounded by the lack of knowledge about human behaviour in schools and the wider world. We all need to know more about the science of the human brain, the mind and the subconscious, and how they control us.

I started to observe people and their thoughts, and how they coped with their problems. I wanted to bring awareness to people about themselves. It was only when

I attended a **Cognitive Behaviour Program** for my mental health, that I truly realized how our mind controls us.

> *'You make your life hard by always being in your head. Life is simple, get out of your head and get into the moment'.*
>
> ***– Sylvester Mcnutt***

As I began implementing what I had learned, my life started to change. This is when I became passionate about sharing this knowledge with people and helping them take control of their lives.

Who wants to have a better life?—we all do! This book is going to help us realize how we have been limiting ourselves and also elaborate on simple steps that can consciously help us overcome unwanted myths, beliefs and biases that are no good to us.

I started my career at the age of forty-three because until then I constantly proclaimed to myself: 'I am not capable of doing any work'. Also, writing this book would not have been possible before that as I never believed that 'I was creative enough'.

I am sure that this book will radically change our beliefs, thoughts and eventually our lives. New opportunities are waiting to be realized.

Start right away! Do not hold back from experiencing a whole new life!

Each chapter provides **secrets** that will help us discover new attributes about ourselves. Let us unshackle and unleash the potential of our minds!

'LIVE CONSCIOUSLY'.

'YOU MUST LEARN A NEW WAY TO THINK FOR A HAPPY LIFE'.

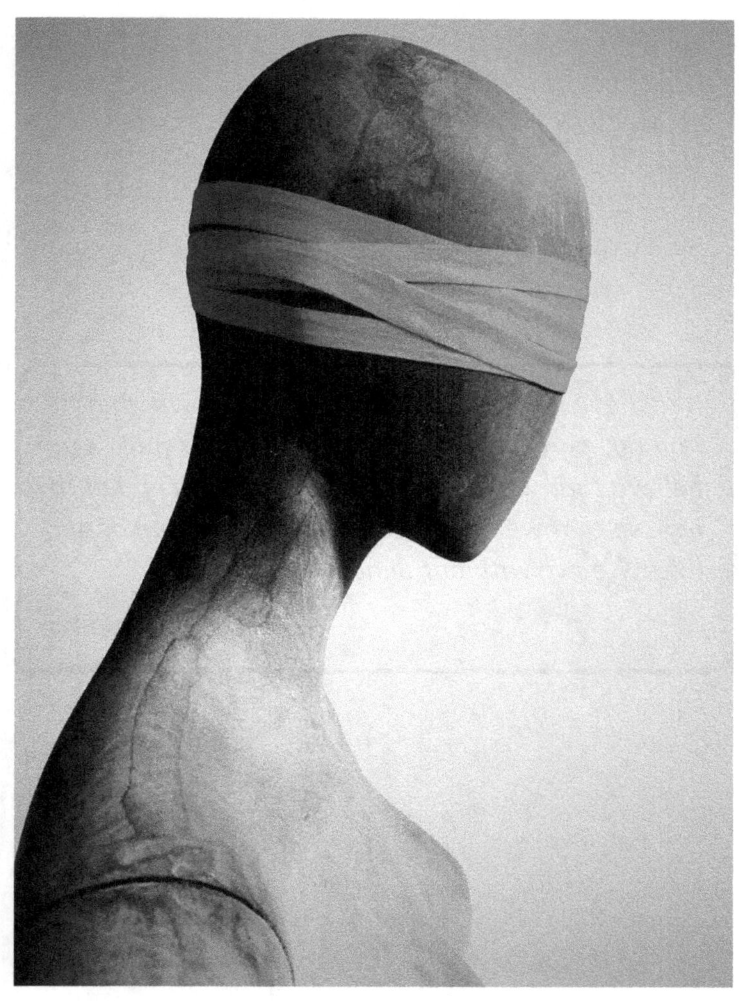

'We have been blindfolded by our own minds. And our perception of the world is what makes us believe that we are helpless. We have been led to believe that we cannot control the direction of our lives; we live with our blindfolds'.

– Pritti M Dhanukka

01

Challenging the Status Quo: Confronting Uncomfortable Truths

Mita was sitting in her kitchen one morning when her husband Sam suddenly came in looking agitated and anxious. He was grumbling about the water heater being left on and the lack of food in the kitchen.

"What's wrong, Sam?" Mita asked gently.

Sam snapped at her, "Nothing", but Mita was not convinced. She stayed where she was and offered him some fruit. "It's okay, you can tell me if you want to", she said.

Sam sighed. "I have a presentation at work today, and I'm afraid I'm going to mess it up", he said. "And then my boss will be angry with me... what if she fires me? I'm such a failure".

Mita shook her head. "Haven't you given great presentations and aced your assignments before?" she asked. Sam had to admit that he had—in fact, his colleagues had even asked him to work with them on an upcoming project.

"So why are you getting so anxious and beating yourself up so much?" Mita continued. "You've done your best with this presentation, so just relax and give it your all".

Sam smiled, thanked Mita, and then went to work. Sam had gained some clarity on his thoughts and was better equipped to handle the situation.

It's important to be aware of our thoughts and let go of unnecessary worries. That way, we can focus on the real problem at hand and find a solution. Self-awareness works in two ways: It helps us to understand ourselves better and those around us as well. This saves us from being judgemental and feeling hurt by the behaviour of others which often seems unfair.

As humans, we are complex and fascinating beings who are capable of creating new worlds through the power of our exponential minds. Despite this incredible potential, we often find ourselves feeling powerless and helpless. This is because we still choose to believe that our lives are shaped by external forces beyond our control.

In truth, however, much of what we experience in life is shaped by our thoughts, behaviours and decisions. Our perceptions of the world around us can either limit or empower us, depending on how we choose to view them.

> *'Your mind-set matters. It affects everything—from the business and investment decisions you make to the way you raise your children, to your stress levels and overall well-being'.*
>
> ***– Peter Diamandis***

If your mind-set and perceptions are so important, why do you often feel like you are living in a world shaped by your own biases and illusions?

According to famous psychologist and author Daniel Kahneman, '*We can be blind to the obvious, and we can also be blind to our blindness*'. In other words, we may not even be aware of the thoughts and beliefs that are holding us back from achieving our true potential.

Welcome to **The Blindfold**, a book about finding our true selves by removing the veil of myths, beliefs and thoughts from our minds.

Have you ever felt like something was holding you back: like there was a barrier preventing you from reaching your full potential? Well, that barrier is the blindfold, and it's about time you remove it.

The blindfold is the collection of myths, beliefs and thoughts that we hold onto without ever questioning them. They are the assumptions we make about the world and ourselves, the stories we tell ourselves and the fears that hold us back. They create a veil that prevents us from seeing the truth.

Are you aware that your perceptions and decision-making processes are influenced in countless ways? They prevent us from taking risks, pursuing our passions and living authentically. They keep us stuck in the same patterns of behaviour and hold us back from reaching our full potential.

> *'The greatest discovery of my generation is that a human being can alter his life by altering his attitude'.*
>
> ***– William James***

The Blindfold is not just another self-help book, it is rather a call to action for those who want to take control of their lives and live genuinely. I will be sharing practical strategies and insights that will help us break free from the myths, biases and illusions that hold us back and also embrace a new reality.

It is fascinating how we are misguided by our perceptions and beliefs, which limit our potential and prevent us from living fulfilling lives.

This book challenges us to remove our blindfolds and see the world for what it truly is, without any illusions or preconceived notions. This requires courage, honesty and a willingness to confront uncomfortable truths about ourselves and the world around us.

> *'Removing the blindfold can be a daunting and uncomfortable process. It might challenge our beliefs and shake the foundations of our identity. But in doing so, we'll discover a new sense of clarity, purpose and meaning'.*
>
> ***– Pritti M Dhanukka***

There are practical strategies that can help us reclaim our lives by breaking us free from societal norms and cultural conditioning, which are known to shape our interpretations and influence our decisions.

We have the power to control the direction of our lives and to create the future we want.

What if you could truly understand how your decisions are affecting your lives and also make choices that would help you reach your goals?

The reality is that we can make this possible. We can make decisions that will help us reach our goals and live a life that we are truly proud of.

'It's time to take off the blindfold and embrace the world for what it is'.

– Pritti M Dhanukka

'The journey starts here. Let's embark on this adventure together and unlock the full potential of our lives'.

– Pritti M Dhanukka

'We learn our belief systems as very little children, and then we move through life creating experiences to match our beliefs. Look back in your own lives and notice how often you have gone through the same experience'.

– Louise L. Hay

Note to Self

02

The Mind's Tricks: The Biases You Don't See

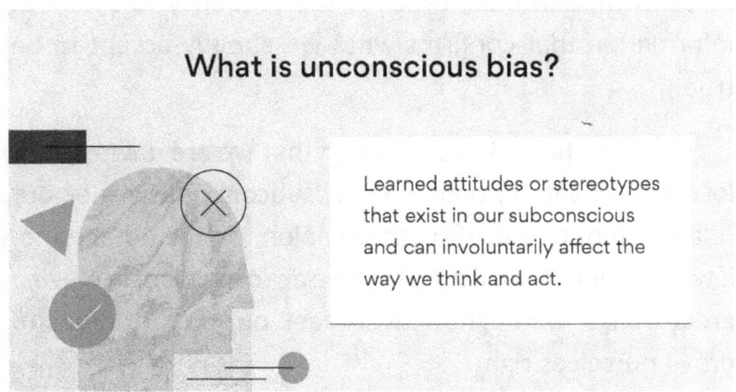

As humans, we all have **biases**, which are systematic errors in thinking or judgement that can influence our perceptions, beliefs and decision-making. They can arise from various sources, such as cultural and social norms, personal experiences and cognitive processes. Biases are the myths through which we view the world, and they shape the way we interpret and respond to our experiences. From a young age, we are taught what to believe and how to behave by the people around us, such as our parents, caregivers and other influential adults.

It is essentially a set of values, ideas and assumptions that we hold to be true. It influences everything, from the decisions we make to the way we give meaning to events and situations.

One of the most interesting things about our convictions is that they tend to be self-reinforcing. In other words, we create experiences in our lives that match our existing convictions. This is often referred to as **confirmation bias**, which is the tendency to seek out information that confirms what we already accept to be true.

If we embrace the conviction that we are unworthy of love and attention, then we may subconsciously seek out relationships that confirm this opinion. On the other hand, if we accept the conviction that we are capable of achieving great things, we might actively seek out opportunities to prove ourselves right.

This can be either good or bad. On one hand, our convictions motivate us to achieve great things and push past our limitations. But there may be instances when it can also hold us back and prevent us from seeking opportunities that may not align with our existing beliefs. It is generally seen to be influential.

As we grow older, we may encounter new experiences that challenge our existing philosophy. For example, if we are taught to accept that failure is a sign of weakness, then we may become fearful of taking risks or trying new things. However, if we have an experience that shows us that failure can be a valuable learning opportunity, then we may begin to challenge and adjust our convictions accordingly.

The myths can also impact our behaviour in subtle ways that we may not even be aware of. For example: if we believe that we are not good enough, then we may unconsciously sabotage ourselves or avoid opportunities that could lead to success. If we believe that we are always right, then we may live in denial of anything beyond our knowledge which again makes us poor listeners as we close ourselves to learning and accepting new ideas.

Confirmation bias is the tendency to seek out information that confirms our existing beliefs while ignoring information that contradicts them. If a person is sceptical of vaccines, then he may search for information that confirms his belief that vaccines are dangerous, ignoring information that suggests otherwise. He may read articles and watch videos that support his position on the subject, all the while dismissing opposing views even if they appear to be scientifically sound.

This bias can cause us to fall into an echo chamber that validates our opinions. Imagine a person who has grown up in a community where he has been taught that people from a certain ethnic group are not trustworthy. This person may come to believe that this group of people is inherently dishonest or even dangerous, without ever having had any direct, negative experiences with individuals from the said group. This belief is based on cultural conditioning rather than objective truth. However, if this person gets to interact with someone from that ethnic group and has a positive experience, then their beliefs may begin to shift. They may begin to realize that their previous opinion was based on incomplete or biased information. They may also come to believe that people from the said ethnic group are just as diverse and complex as anyone else.

Our convictions are not always based on objective reality. As such, it is important to recognize that our beliefs may not always reflect the truth of a situation.

The **Negative Bias** is yet another notion that shapes our convictions. This gives rise to pessimism which can limit our ability to see opportunities for growth and success.

Imagine a person who is starting a new job. What if they tend to focus on the challenges and difficulties they might face rather than the opportunities for growth and learning? Then this negative bias may cause them to feel overwhelmed and anxious, leading to a self-fulfilling prophecy of failure.

Another strong conviction is the **Conformity Bias**. Since childhood, we are tamed by several societal norms. This instils a fear of non-acceptance by the people around us if we behave differently from others in our society. It is the tendency to conform to the opinions and behaviours of others in our social group, even if they conflict with our personal beliefs. This bias is rooted in a fear of rejection or disapproval from others, which can limit our ability to think and act independently.

It so often happens that in a group of friends who are all interested in a particular hobby, one member might not share this interest. They may feel pressure to conform to the group's opinion and participate in the hobby, rather than express their preferences.

Many times young adults indulge in substance abuse and other practices just to feel accepted and qualified within their peer group.

The **Hindsight Bias** is the tendency to believe that we would have predicted the outcome of an event after it has occurred, even if we had no prior knowledge or information about the event. This bias can cause us to overestimate our ability to predict the future and underestimate the role of chance or other factors in determining outcomes.

A person watching a sports game may believe that they knew which team was going to win all along, even if they did not predict it before the game started.

The **Self-Serving Bias** is the tendency to attribute our successes to our abilities and efforts while attributing our failures to external factors beyond our control. As a result, we tend to overestimate our abilities and develop a lack of accountability for our mistakes.

Let us consider a student who receives a good grade on an exam. They may attribute their success to their own intelligence and hard work, rather than acknowledging the role of luck or other external factors in their performance. On the other hand, if the student receives a bad grade then they may blame the teacher for setting a difficult exam, rather than taking responsibility for their lack of preparation.

I have closely seen many people investing in stocks who strongly abide by this bias. When they successfully close good profits from their stock holding, they give their calculative mind all the credit. However, if they incur losses then they will blame the agent or other factors for it.

Self-Serving Bias holds us back from taking ownership of our failures as we may do for our achievements.

Another type of bias that has been studied extensively is the **Halo effect**, which is the tendency to judge a person positively in one area based on their perceived positive qualities in another area. A study found that people rated a job candidate as more competent when they were described as physically attractive, even though their appearance was unrelated to their actual job performance.

There is another staunch conviction that needs to be challenged for healthy relationships, namely **Gender Bias.**

This particular bias is the most detrimental when it comes to the relationship between spouses. It has been observed that no matter how successful a person is, how appealing and acceptable they might be in society, they are viewed in a completely different light by their spouses. In most societies, even today, men consider themselves to be the supreme authority and decision-makers in their worth. The wives still struggle for acceptance and respect; they also harbour a desire to refrain from age-old stereotypes.

Understanding Gender Bias: How can it affect your perception and distort reality?

The way we think about gender can have a huge impact on how we perceive reality and interact with others. From stereotypes to self-fulfilling prophecies, gender bias can lead to unfair treatment and distorted views of people based on their gender. In this section, we will explore how gender bias can affect our perception and distort reality in several ways.

Stereotyping

Gender bias gives rise to stereotyping, where we categorize people based on their gender and make assumptions about their behaviours, interests and abilities. As a result, we may develop a distorted view of reality where people are seen as fitting into narrow and limiting gender roles. This can have a damaging effect on those who do not fit into these limited roles, in other words, those people who are simply different from the norm.

Stereotypes can lead us to make assumptions about someone's capabilities and interests that may not be accurate. For example, we may assume that a woman is less capable of pursuing a career in a traditionally male-dominated field, or that a man is not interested in cooking or taking care of children. These assumptions can limit our understanding of a person's capabilities and interests and lead us to make unfair judgements of them.

Confirmation Bias

Gender bias can also lead to confirmation bias, where we tend to seek out and remember information that confirms our existing beliefs about gender. This can lead us to ignore evidence that contradicts our biases and reinforce our distorted views of reality. As a result, we make assumptions about someone's abilities or interests based on their gender, rather than focusing on actual evidence.

For example, if a woman expresses an interest in a traditionally male-dominated field, we may be more likely to remember instances that confirm our beliefs that women are not suited to that field, and further ignore evidence that contradicts our assumptions. As a result, we may develop unfair and inaccurate judgements of someone's capabilities and interests.

Self-Fulfilling Prophecy

Gender bias can create a self-fulfilling prophecy, where our biases lead us to treat people differently based on their gender. This can influence people's behaviour and performance, leading them to conform to the stereotypes we hold about their gender. For example, if a woman is constantly told that she is not suitable for a particular career, she may become discouraged and give up on pursuing it.

Eventually, we may develop a distorted view of reality, where people are seen as fitting into limited gender roles and are discouraged from pursuing interests outside of those roles. People who do not conform to such stereotypes may be subjected to unfair treatment and loss of opportunities.

Attribution Bias

Gender bias can also lead to attribution bias, where we attribute different causes to the behaviour of men and women. For example, we may attribute a man's success to his skills and abilities, while attributing a woman's success to luck or external factors. This can distort our view of reality and lead to unfair treatment of people based on their gender.

This is often seen in the workplace where men are often given more credit for their successes than women. As a result, we may come to believe that women are less capable than men and are less likely to be given opportunities for advancement.

Gender bias can have a profound impact on our perception of reality and how we interact with others. It can lead to unfair treatment, stereotypes and distorted views of people based on their gender. It is important to recognize and challenge these biases to create a more equitable and just society.

Some prevalent gender biases influencing our outlook are listed below:

- 'Women are emotional and irrational'.
- 'Men are strong and aggressive'.
- 'Women are better at nurturing and caring'.
- 'Men are better at leadership and decision making'.
- 'Women are not as capable as men in technical fields'.
- 'Men are not as good as women in caring fields'.

- 'Women are not as competitive as men'.
- 'Men are not as empathetic as women'.
- 'Women are too sensitive'.
- 'Men are too aggressive'.
- 'Women are too emotional to be in positions of power'.
- 'Men are the primary breadwinners'.
- 'Women are too weak to handle physical tasks'.
- 'Men are better at negotiating'.
- 'Women are too caring to be tough leaders'.
- 'Men are too logical to understand emotions'.
- 'Women are not as ambitious as men'.
- 'Men are not as nurturing as women'.

By understanding how gender bias can affect our perception and distort reality, we can begin to recognize and challenge our own biases. We can strive to create a more impartial society where everyone is treated with respect and given the same opportunities regardless of their gender.

Overall, biases can be subtle and difficult to detect and they can impact our decision-making in ways that we may not even be aware of. By understanding these biases and being aware of our tendencies to develop a bias we can make more informed and equitable decisions. By questioning our biases, we can open ourselves up to new experiences and opportunities. We can learn to see the world in a new way and overcome limitations that we thought were holding us back.

Let us keep peeling off the layers of the fold furthermore until we uncover the treasures of our unique reality. In the next chapter, we will delve into how we have been tuned to instinctive thinking since our evolution.

Note to Self

03

The Foundation of Your Reality

As a twin born prematurely, I was kept under observation in an incubator away from my mother. I spent my early childhood with my family, playing and learning about the world around me. I was a happy-go-lucky child, always looking for the next adventure or game to play. However, life can be unpredictable and my family soon found themselves facing significant changes.

My father started a business and we moved to a new house in a bustling metropolis with an entirely different way of life. The excitement of starting a new chapter in our lives was tempered by the challenges that came with moving to an unfamiliar place.

As we adjusted to our new surroundings, I began to notice changes in the behaviour of my family members. They became more protective, constantly on the lookout for potential threats and dangers. Even as a child, I could sense the unease that had crept into our lives.

It was not until much later in life that I came to understand the root cause of these changes.

As a twin born into a world of competition, my **survival instinct** was predominant. This hardwired response to the unknown triggered a protective shield over my innocent, fun-loving self, securing it from painful experiences.

My family's response to our move was a natural result of this survival instinct, the desire to protect their child from harm in a new and unfamiliar environment. However, the unintended consequences of this protective shield are significant.

As I was growing up, I found myself struggling to connect with others. I could not open up or become vulnerable before them; the protective shield I created to keep myself safe in the past was now holding me back, limiting my ability to form meaningful connections and experience the joys of life to the fullest.

It was not until I began tracing the origin of my instinctive behaviour and exploring the impact of my thoughts and emotions on my life that I began to break down this protective shield. Through introspection and other behavioural techniques, I learned to control my thoughts and navigate toward a more balanced, positive approach to life.

Today, I look back on my life with a sense of gratitude for the lessons learned. While the hunter instinct may have been predominant in me, it is just one aspect of my complex and multifaceted personality. By acknowledging and understanding this instinct I have been able to develop a more well-rounded approach to life, one that embraces both the joys and challenges of the human experience.

It is observed that we tend to focus more on unpleasant thoughts than pleasant ones. People in general are more worried about things going wrong than right. Well, that is because our brains are hardwired to respond to negative experiences more strongly than positive ones. Humans are biased towards negative thinking which is very deeply rooted in our subconscious from the primitive age.

It's a survival mechanism that evolved in our ancestors. They primarily lived as nomads, which was a hunting-based existence. This way of life was riskier, with greater uncertainty and potential danger. The survival instinct developed as a response to the unknown and potentially dangerous circumstances of the hunter–gatherer lifestyle. The mind was always on high alert and very reactive to situations. Our ancestors had to be vigilant for danger all the time. They needed to be ready to react quickly to threats like a Sabre-toothed tiger jumping out from behind a tree. So they had to be on guard all the time. They always assumed the worst-case scenario and were ready to act. This led to the development of the fighter instinct where our brains are more attuned to negative stimuli than positive ones.

Positive emotions are not as essential for survival as negative ones. For example, being happy did not necessarily help our ancestors avoid danger or secure resources. So, positive emotions took a backseat to negative ones in terms of importance.

Though we no longer have to worry about being attacked by ferocious animals, our brains still carry over this protective instinct into our modern world. Hence we tend to react more strongly to undesirable situations than to positive ones. The negativity bias is a coping mechanism against emotional attacks. It helps us to be more prepared for potential threats, even if they do not exist. But it's important to recognize that our brains are wired this way and hence we have to make an effort to focus on healthy experiences too. This can help balance out our emotions and improve our overall well-being.

Our mind can easily guide us toward negative thoughts, especially when we are having a busy day. The stress and pressures of daily life can trigger our ancient survival instincts, leading us to perceive potential threats or dangers in our environment.

Even minor incidents, like someone bumping into us in a store, can elicit negative thoughts and emotions that reflect this instinctual response. Imagine shopping in a crowded grocery store and accidentally bumping into someone with our cart. As we continue on our way, we may find ourselves feeling angry or frustrated with the other person, even if it was just a minor collision. One undesirable experience leads to another and we get stuck in a swirl of negativity.

Our mind may start to focus on the negative aspects of the situation, such as the annoyance of having to navigate around other people in a crowded store or the fact that the other person was not paying attention, or that they caused the collision in the first place. We may start to form negative judgements about the other person's character, questioning their intelligence and capabilities—'Why did that person have to bump into me? Can't they watch where they're going? What's wrong with them?' This negative way of thinking sets off a chain reaction in our bodies. The blood pressure might rise and we might start to tense up or shake our heads. These physical behaviours then trigger a flood of emotions and physiological changes like an increased heartbeat among others. We might feel irritated, frustrated or even angry.

These negative thoughts can quickly snowball and affect our mood and behaviour for the rest of the day. We may find ourselves feeling more irritable or frustrated, or even start to avoid situations that could trigger similar negative reactions.

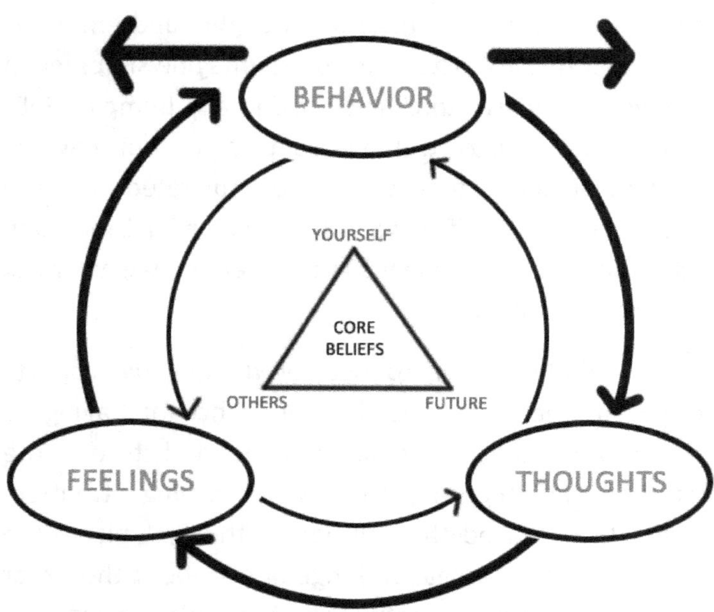

It's fascinating to think about how our thoughts, behaviours and emotions are all interconnected.

This has a significant impact on our lives. When we allow negative thoughts to snowball they can have a domino effect on our actions and emotions, affecting everything from our relationships to our work and overall well-being.

Consciously choosing to focus on positive thoughts and emotions, we can break the cycle of negativity and improve our overall well-being. What if we choose to think about the situation differently? Instead of feeling endangered and thinking the worst about the person we bumped into, we can decide to give them the benefit of the doubt. 'Maybe it was an accident, or perhaps they're having a bad day too. Maybe it was just a mistake, no harm done'. In such cases, our reaction to the situation is much more positive. We might even smile at the person. This releases some feel-good hormones like serotonin.

And here's where it gets really interesting. Once we have a healthy thought, it then leads to more positive thoughts and emotions. Suppose we start thinking about a similar experience when our grandmother stumbled upon us at a store. Suddenly the annoying person does not seem like such a big deal anymore. The highly cautious brain puts its armour down. Our whole mood has shifted, just because we chose to think a little differently and feel secure.

It's not easy to recondition our thought patterns, but with practice and patience, we can cultivate a more positive mind-set that supports our mental and emotional health in modern-day living.

As with all things in life, balance is the key.

> *'Negative thinking patterns can be immensely deceptive and persuasive, and change is rarely easy. But with patience and persistence, I believe that nearly all individuals suffering from depression can improve and experience a sense of joy and self-esteem once again'.*
>
> ***– David D. Burns***

Note to Self

04

The Impulse to Control: Harnessing Your Instincts for Positive Change

One evening, an old Cherokee chief was teaching his grandson about life. He told the boy, “Inside each of us, two wolves are fighting for control. One is filled with anger, envy, jealousy and negativity. The other is filled with love, kindness, compassion and positivity”.

The boy thought about this for a moment and then asked his grandfather, "Which wolf will win?"

The chief replied, "The one you feed".

We have to be aware of the importance of managing our instincts and behaviours in a way that promotes positive growth and self-worth. By choosing to feed the wolf that embodies love, kindness, compassion and positivity, we can cultivate healthy relationships and lead a fulfilling life.

On the other hand, when we give in to our negative instincts and behaviours we risk feeding the wolf that embodies anger, envy, jealousy and negativity. This can lead to self-doubt, destructive behaviour and damaged relationships.

We have the power to choose which wolf we feed. By recognizing and managing our thoughts and actions in a way that promotes positive growth and healthy relationships, we can achieve our full potential and lead fulfilling lives.

The miracle of human life is a fascinating phenomenon that never ceases to amaze us. From the moment we are conceived in the womb, we embark on a journey filled with incredible transformations and adaptations. However, perhaps the most remarkable aspect about us is the treasure trove that lies within our brains.

As we make the transition from the safety of the womb to the real world, we are equipped with a set of innate survival instincts. These include the ability to seek instant gratification for our basic needs, such as hunger and comfort.

Unfortunately, if we fail to evolve and grow out of these instincts as we mature, we may encounter various challenges in life. We may struggle with mistrust, anger and frustration, hindering our ability to form meaningful relationships and achieve our goals.

Have you noticed how a child clings to the crib with a firm grip, even from birth? This instinct is crucial for their survival and ensures that they feel secure in their environment. Similarly, when a new-born feels something touching their cheek, they instinctively turn their head and begin to suckle, thus fulfilling their hunger.

These innate behaviours continue to shape our lives as we grow older. By understanding and harnessing them, we can learn to live our lives to the fullest potential. So let us embrace the power of our instincts and use them to fuel our growth and success.

Our innate survival instincts have a significant impact on our thinking patterns and decision-making processes. They influence the way we perceive the world around us and the way we react to different situations.

This instinct to seek instant gratification can sometimes lead us to make impulsive decisions that may not be in our best interests in the long term. Similarly, our survival instinct may cause us to feel anxious or fearful in unfamiliar or threatening situations, even if there is no real danger.

However, by becoming aware of our instincts and learning to manage them, we can improve our thinking and decision-making skills. By taking a step back and analyzing the situation before reacting, we can make more rational and informed choices. We can also learn to recognize when our instincts are not serving us well and find more effective ways to cope with difficult situations.

Understanding the impact of our instincts on our thinking can help us lead more fulfilling and successful lives. We are empowered to make better choices and overcome the obstacles that we face.

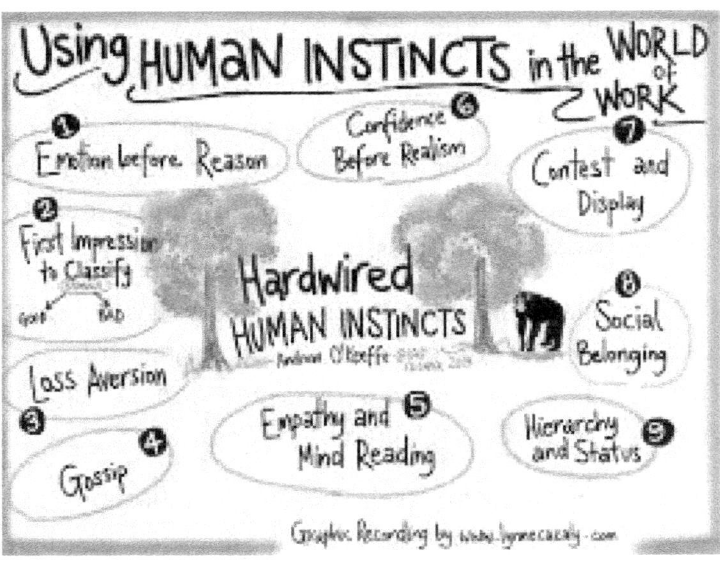

Our innate survival behaviours and instincts can have a significant impact on our self-worth and our behaviour, as well as our interpretation of the situations we go through in life.

The instinct to seek instant gratification can make us feel impatient or frustrated when things do not happen as quickly as we would like. We may then develop feelings of inadequacy or come to believe that we are not good enough to achieve our goals.

Similarly, our survival instinct can cause us to perceive situations as threatening or dangerous, even if they are not. This can lead to anxiety or fear, negatively impacting our behaviour and self-esteem.

The good news is that we can learn to manage them in a way that promotes self-worth and healthy behaviour. By recognizing our strengths and weaknesses and learning to adapt to different situations, we can develop a more positive and confident sense of self.

Note to Self

05

The Shackles of Illusions

> *'Life has no limitations, except the ones you make'.*
>
> ***– Les Brown***

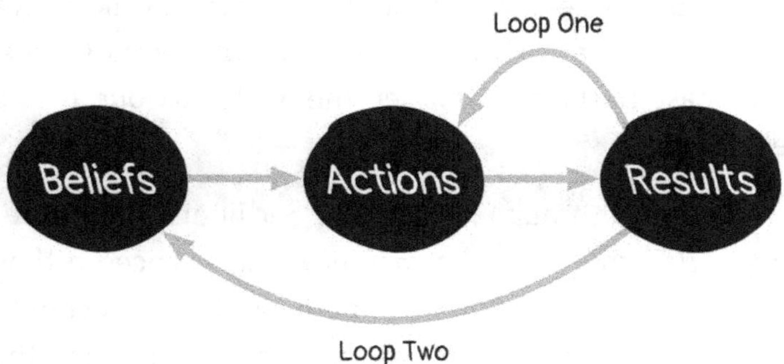

There was a girl named Payal in my school who had a close friend named Veenu. They had been friends for several years and had shared many happy memories. However, one day Payal discovered that Veenu had been talking behind her back and spreading rumours about her. Payal was devastated and felt completely betrayed by someone she had trusted so deeply.

From that point on, Payal began to question all her other relationships. She found it hard to trust anyone and started to distance herself from her other friends and even her partner. She believed that if someone as close as Veenu could betray her, then anyone could do the same.

As time went on, Payal became increasingly isolated and lonely. She began to regret her decision to distance herself from her loved ones but felt that it was too late to go back. It was not until she met a new friend named Lily, who was honest and loyal, that Payal started to regain her trust in others.

Through her experience, Payal learned that while betrayal can be painful and challenging, it's important not to generalize and assume that everyone will behave in the same way. It's crucial to allow ourselves to heal from past hurts and not let them dictate our future relationships.

As we go through life, we use our filters to interpret the world around us. We may have experienced a time when we are engrossed in something like our favourite movie, so much so that we may not even hear the doorbell or other background noise because our focus is elsewhere. Similarly, if there's a loud noise outside that would normally bother us we may not pay attention to it if we are focused on something else. We may generalize certain experiences or delete certain details that do not fit with our preconceived notions. And because each person has their own set of filters, we each create our unique meaning from the information we receive.

Suppose a person was betrayed by a friend or partner in the past. This betrayal may lead the person to develop a belief that true friends or partners do not exist or that they cannot be trusted. As a result, they may start to generalize that all people are untrustworthy.

This belief can then manifest in various ways, such as being overly cautious in new relationships, avoiding social situations or even becoming paranoid. The person may assume that anyone who shows interest in them has ulterior motives and is not to be trusted.

Generalizations

Generalizations are also the mechanisms by which we generate beliefs, which can be helpful or dangerous. They also produce fears: for example, if a dog bites us once then we may have elaborated the belief that all dogs are dangerous.

Such generalizations and beliefs can be harmful as they prevent us from experiencing new relationships and opportunities. It is essential to recognize that one negative experience does not define all future experiences. We should strive to approach each new relationship or situation with an open mind and avoid letting past experiences cloud our judgement.

Sarah was a young girl who was always very anxious and worried about everything. She would often imagine the worst-case scenario and worry about things that are out of her control. One day, she had to attend an important meeting but she was feeling very nervous. As she entered the conference room she noticed that the room was too cold and the chair was uncomfortable, so she could not focus on anything else.

Sarah's anxious thoughts had taken over her perception, and she could not see anything else in the room apart from what was bothering her. She failed to notice the beautiful paintings on the wall, the lovely view outside the window and the friendly faces of her colleagues who were waiting to greet her.

Sarah's experience demonstrates how our anxious thoughts can distort our perception and make us focus on the negative aspects of a situation. This can prevent us from seeing the positive aspects and enjoying the moment. By focusing too much on our worries and anxieties, we can miss out on the good things in life and cause ourselves unnecessary pain and suffering. Therefore, it is important to learn how to manage our anxious thoughts and practice mindfulness: to be conscious of the present moment.

Our minds have a remarkable ability to filter and prioritize the information that we receive. To focus on what we deem most important, we often delete or ignore other perceptions. During non-critical moments, we may even delete up to 80% of the data reaching our brains.

However, when we are anxious this filtering mechanism can become problematic. We may develop tunnel vision and solely focus on the negative aspects of a situation, deleting any positive elements. Suppose a person at a gathering does not like us, we may solely focus on that individual rather than the remaining twenty or so people who do like us.

A friend of mine once told me about how she was uncomfortable around a particular relative. She would avoid going to events where she knew that the relative would be present. But was it the relative who was making her uncomfortable, or was it her perception of the person? This is an important question to consider. Our perceptions, values and beliefs shape our experiences and can influence how we interpret the actions of others. In this case, it is possible that my friend's discomfort was not caused solely by the relative's actions but by her interpretation of them.

Mary had always been a hard-working student, consistently getting good grades and putting in extra effort to excel in her studies. One day she received a 'B grade' on a test, which was lower than her usual grades. Immediately she began to personalize the situation, thinking that her teacher must have graded her harshly because she did not like Mary or that her classmates must be smarter than her.

Mary's thoughts began to consume her, and she became anxious about her abilities as a student. She began to compare herself with her classmates. She also tried to find flaws in their work just so that she could feel better. However, this only made her more anxious and critical of herself.

One day her teacher wanted to speak with her after class. Mary assumed the worst and thought that her teacher was going to criticize her for her poor grades. However, to her surprise, her teacher commended her for her hard work and dedication to her studies.

Mary realized that she had been personalizing the situation and projecting her insecurities onto her teacher and classmates. She learned that not everything is a direct reaction to her actions and that her perception can distort the reality of a situation. From that day on, Mary tried to be more aware of her thoughts and not personalize situations that may not have anything to do with her.

Samantha worked in a large corporate office with dozens of other employees. She had always prided herself on her work ethic and her ability to get things done efficiently. One day, however, she received an email from her boss that left her feeling angry and frustrated.

The email said that there had been a delay in one of the projects that Samantha was working on, and that the delay was causing problems for other teams in the office. Samantha immediately took the email personally, assuming that her boss was blaming her for the delay and suggesting that she was not doing her job properly.

Samantha spent the next few days feeling upset and anxious about the email, and she started to question her abilities and worth as an employee. She became convinced that her boss was disappointed in her, and that she was going to be fired for her supposed incompetence.

As it turned out, the delay in the project was not caused by Samantha's actions. There had been a miscommunication between her team and another team in the office which had led to the delay. But because Samantha had personalized the situation and assumed that her boss's email was directed solely at her, she had created a great deal of unnecessary stress and self-doubt for herself.

Eventually, Samantha realized that she had been taking things too personally and had been unfairly blaming herself for something that was not entirely her fault. She learned to take a step back and objectively evaluate situations before automatically assuming that they are personal attacks against her.

Personalization

Personalization is a filter that people use to create meaning from the information they receive. When we personalize things, we believe that everything that others say or do is a direct personal reaction to us. We compare ourselves to other people and we try to give the impression that we are smarter, better looking and more intelligent than others.

However, this way of thinking can cause us to feel responsible for events that we cannot control. This kind of thinking is a significant trigger for self-blame.

Another example is when an individual feels responsible for whether other people have a good time when they are with them. They may think, 'If only I had done this or that, then the incident would not have happened'.

When we get to understand this model of thought, it adds flexibility to our communication. It helps us to relate better to different personality types, even ones that we found challenging in the past, and to be more mindful and alert.

There is a simple way of identifying the filters we have been using thus far. We can pick up any incident from the past to review where filters kicked in. Did we interpret the information in a healthy or unhealthy way? How else could we have interpreted the same information?

Information processing in the human brain is a complex process. Several other filters will be addressed in my upcoming book -

 # Filters - Information tagging in our mind.

However, it's important to question this kind of thinking and realize that we cannot control everything. While we can influence some people in some ways, we can only control how we choose to react or respond to the circumstances and situations we encounter.

In the next chapter, we will explore how our beliefs shape or destroy us and our realities.

Note to Self

06

The Lies You Tell Yourself: Recognizing and Releasing Limiting Beliefs

'Our beliefs about what we are and what we can be precisely determine what we can be'.

– Tony Robbins

Our beliefs shape our reality. If we believe that we cannot do something, we would not even try, and therefore we will fail by default. If we believe that we can, then we are more likely to take action and succeed.

Wilma Rudolph was an American sprinter who was born prematurely and suffered from numerous illnesses as a child, including pneumonia and scarlet fever. When she was five years old she contracted polio which left her with a limp and a leg brace.

Despite her physical challenges, Wilma had a strong belief in her ability to overcome her limitations and pursue her dream of becoming an athlete. She began working with a physical therapist and eventually learned to walk without her brace. She began running and by the age of thirteen, she had joined her school's track team.

Wilma faced numerous challenges on her journey to becoming an Olympic champion. She faced discrimination due to her race and gender and was told that she would never be able to compete at the highest level of athletics. However, she refused to let these limiting beliefs hold her back.

At the 1960 Olympic Games, Wilma won three gold medals setting world records in the 100-meter, 200-meter and 4x100-meter relay events. She became a symbol of perseverance and determination, inspiring people around the world to overcome their limitations and pursue their dreams.

Wilma's story illustrates how our beliefs shape our reality. Despite facing numerous obstacles, Wilma had a strong belief in her ability to overcome her limitations and pursue her dream. This belief gave her the motivation and courage to work hard and push through her challenges. If she had believed in the limiting beliefs set by others—that she was too weak, too sickly, too disadvantaged—then she would have never become the Olympic champion she is today.

Wilma Rudolph shows us that our beliefs shape our reality. If we believe in ourselves and our ability to overcome our limitations, then we can achieve great things. However, if we allow limiting beliefs to hold us back, then we will never reach our full potential. The choice is ours—we can either believe that we can or believe that we cannot, but as Henry Ford said, 'we're right' either way.

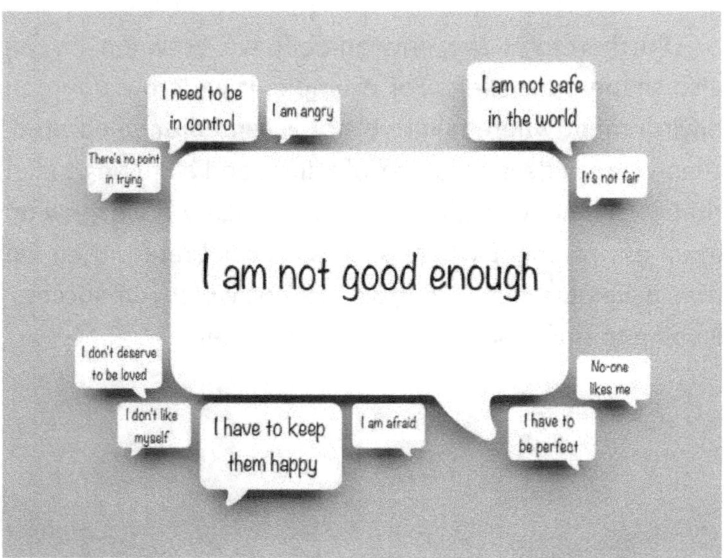

Limiting beliefs are self-imposed barriers. According to a study published in the Journal of Personality and Social Psychology, adverse childhood experiences such as abuse, neglect and trauma can lead to negative beliefs about oneself and the world, leading to low self-esteem, depression and anxiety. Additionally, the study found that positive childhood experiences, such as feeling loved and supported, can give rise to positive beliefs and a healthy sense of self.

Culture and environment also play a role in shaping our limiting beliefs. A study published in the Journal of Cross-Cultural Psychology states that cultural factors can influence beliefs about success, failure and self-worth. For example, in some cultures, success is defined by academic achievement, while in others success is defined by financial prosperity. These cultural beliefs can lead to limiting beliefs about one's abilities and potential.

Furthermore, the environment we grow up in can also shape our beliefs. For example, if we grow up in an environment where failure is not accepted or celebrated, then we may develop a fear of failure and a limiting belief that we are not capable of success. Similarly, if we grow up in an environment where success is celebrated, then we may develop a belief that we are not worthy of success, leading to self-sabotage and limiting beliefs.

Some common limiting beliefs are:

'I'm not good enough'

A person may develop this limiting belief after experiencing repeated failures or negative feedback from others. For example, a student who struggles academically may start to believe that they are not smart enough to succeed. Similarly, someone who experiences rejection or criticism in their personal or professional life may start to believe that they are not worthy of love or success.

'I don't deserve to be successful'

This limiting belief can stem from feelings of guilt or unworthiness. For example, a person who has made mistakes in the past may believe that they do not deserve to achieve their goals or be successful. Similarly, someone who has grown up in a culture or environment that places a strong emphasis on humility and self-sacrifice may develop a belief that pursuing personal success is selfish or immoral.

'Money is evil'

This limiting belief can develop as a result of cultural or societal conditioning. When someone grows up in a community that emphasizes modesty and simplicity, they may develop a belief that wealth and material possessions are bad or immoral. Similarly, someone who has experienced financial hardship or inequality may develop a belief that money is the root of all evil and should be avoided.

'I'm stuck in my circumstances'

This limiting belief can develop when a person feels trapped or powerless in their current situation. If someone is struggling with addiction or mental illness, they may believe that they are unable to change their circumstances or overcome their challenges. Similarly, someone who has experienced significant setbacks or failures may start to believe that they are unable to achieve their goals or create a better life for themselves.

'I'm too old/young'

This limiting belief can develop as a result of societal or cultural norms around age and achievement. It's often noticed that young people who are told that they are not yet experienced enough to pursue a certain career or goal may start to believe that they are indeed too young to succeed. Similarly, older people who are told that they are past their prime may develop a belief that they are too old to make significant changes in their lives or pursue new opportunities.

Some of our beliefs form myths, which are stories that we tell ourselves about how the world works, and they often have no basis in reality. Yet we hold onto them and they become part of the blindfold that prevents us from seeing the truth. The following myths can affect our lives and decisions in many ways:

- 'Success only comes to those who are lucky';
- 'I'm not good enough to achieve my goals';
- 'I'm not worthy of love and happiness';
- 'Failure is a reflection of my worth as a person'.

Which of the above beliefs do you own for yourself?

Myths can hold us back from taking risks, pursuing our dreams and living genuinely. So, how can we identify and overcome these myths?

It is essential to recognize and challenge our limiting beliefs and work to overcome them for a desired life. According to experts, challenging our limiting beliefs can lead to positive changes in behaviour and mind-set. The study found that when participants were asked to reflect on their limiting beliefs and challenge them, they were more likely to take action toward their goals and experience a sense of empowerment.

Note to Self

07

Rewriting Your Story: Escaping the Trap of Thoughts

'Whether you think you can or you think you can't—you're right'.

– Henry Ford

We all have thoughts that tend to be so automatic that we do not question or challenge them: 'I'll never be able to find a job that I love because I'm not exceptional at anything', 'It must be my fault that they don't like me because there's something wrong with me', 'Nothing works for me: my life is never going to change'. It's amazing when we stop and think about how many negative thoughts go through our minds each day.

It is important to become aware of such devastating thoughts that lead us to have misguiding beliefs about ourselves and our situations. Specialists have been able to identify that a large part of anxiety is either due to personal issues from the past or the habit of making false assumptions and predictions about events in the future. The mind tends to predict that a situation will go poorly, when in fact there is no evidence to support the prediction.

This habit can be very effectively dealt with by a straightforward process which is known as the **Thought Record**. What's different about this process is that it can be used by anyone, anywhere.

The Thought Record

The **Thought Record** has been very helpful for me in reframing my automatic thoughts. When we start writing our assumptions, the brain becomes aware and conscious of the quality of our thoughts. The more we use it, the easier it is to fill out and catch the negative thoughts in the process. Once we practice this method for some time, our brain automatically gets tuned in to using it mentally whenever it finds us in the middle of an anxiety-provoking situation.

In this activity we just need to record the following:

1. What is the situation or event that triggers us to think in an unwanted manner?
2. How do we feel when we think about that situation or event?
3. What are the negative thoughts behind our feelings?
4. Identify the past references that support these thoughts.
5. Think of the evidence that contradicts these thoughts.
6. Think of a counterstatement to support our stand against these unpleasant thoughts.

Now, after following the steps we will feel much calmer and in better control of ourselves to be able to work differently and effectively.

Let us see how we can work this out through a simple example:

- ***Situation/trigger:** Briefly describe the situation that led to these unpleasant feelings.

  For example, work presentation.

- ***Feelings:** What do we feel?—Anxiety, guilt, doubt, fear, etc.

- ***Unhelpful thoughts/images***:* Identify the negative thinking (or 'hot thought') behind these feelings.

  For example: 'My presentation is going to go horribly and my boss is going to think that I'm bad at my job. I'm a failure'.

- ***Facts that support the thought***:* Find evidence that supports these unhelpful thoughts.

  For example, 'My boss has told me in the past that she's disappointed with my presentation skills' and 'I didn't prepare as much as I should have'.

- ***Facts that do not support the thought***:* Facts that provide evidence against these unhelpful thoughts.

  For example, 'I have worked on my presentation skills since my poor review and I have improved'; 'I'm not a failure and I'm doing my best' and 'Everyone has bad days at work'.

- ***Think of an alternative/more balanced thought:** Now that we have considered the facts, let us write down a healthier way of thinking.

  For example: 'While I have struggled with presentations before, I've practised and prepared for this presentation and have no proof that this will not go well'.

- ***Re-rate how we feel**—less anxious, calmer and reassured.

This is just one small example that it can be used for, but it can be applied to so many different types of situations, thoughts and personal struggles. It's a really helpful tool to use for body image issues because many of us tend to have automatic negative thoughts about our bodies that can impact our entire day. Sometimes all we need to do is to re-frame our thoughts and move on with our day.

Of course, it takes a bit of practice to be able to reframe a thought (and find evidence that does not support it), but it will get easier over time. Also, not every thought record that we do is going to be life-changing, but I can attest to how impactful it can be.

The first time I did the thought record with my therapist, I had this major 'a-ha' moment. She helped me write a more balanced thought (I actually could not think of one, so she filled one out for me) and it brought me to tears because something just clicked inside of me. It was amazing how it helped me see a situation in a new light that I had never thought about before. That one moment has had a huge impact on how I think about myself and my life today.

The Thought Record makes my thoughts more realistic and balanced when anxiety tends to stir up. The practice may help us slow down or stop those automatic thoughts in their tracks. I can 'catch' them fairly quickly now, recognize them for what they are and realize that my thinking is not realistic or fair. It sure beats going along in life and accepting every negative thought that comes to mind.

When we feel stuck on an issue, we can try using the Thought Record. It may just help us see something in a new way.

Get access, for the ease of practice, to a downloadable Thought Record for yourself on my site http://www.lifecoachpritti.com/thoughtrecord

Thought Record

Situation	Thoughts	Emotions	Behaviors	Alternate Thought

Note to Self

08

Breaking the Chains of Confirmation and Negativity Bias: How to Overcome Your Mind's Limitations

'The truth will set you free, but first, it will piss you off'.

– Gloria Steinem

Break this cycle by changing the way we think about things. If we can catch ourselves having a negative thought and reframe it more positively, then we can change our behaviour and our emotions too. It's not always easy, of course. Our brains are wired to look for threats and problems, so it takes some effort to override that instinct. But with practice, it can become a habit.

One way to practice this is to keep a thought diary. Whenever we notice ourselves having a negative thought, write it down and then try to reframe it more positively. For example, if we find ourselves thinking 'I'm such a failure', then we could try thinking 'I'm not perfect, but I'm doing the best I can'. Over time, we will start to notice patterns in our thinking process and develop the ability to challenge those negative thoughts more easily.

So, the next time a frustrating experience comes up try to remember that our thoughts can have a powerful impact on how we feel. By choosing to think positively, we can break the cycle of negativity and start to feel better. It's not a magic cure process, but it can be a helpful tool in improving our mood and overall well-being.

I once had a friend who was always stressed out and anxious about everything. She would constantly complain about her job, her finances and her relationships. One day, we were out shopping together and a man accidentally bumped into her while reaching for an item on the shelf. She immediately turned around and snapped at him, "Watch where you're going, buddy!" The man looked embarrassed and quickly walked away.

I noticed that my friend was still fuming about the incident, so I tried to encourage her to think about the situation differently. I asked her, "What if that man was just having a bad day? Maybe he's dealing with some personal issues that we know nothing about. Do you think you could find it in your heart to forgive him?"

At first, my friend was resistant to the idea. But as we continued to talk, she began to soften and see things from a different perspective. She realized that her negative thoughts were only making her feel worse and that by choosing to think positively she could break the cycle of negativity and start to feel better.

By the end of our conversation, my friend was feeling more relaxed and even had a smile on her face. She said, "You know what? You're right. Maybe that guy was just having a bad day. I shouldn't have snapped at him like that. I'm going to try to be more mindful of my thoughts from now on".

From that day forward, I noticed a significant shift in my friend's attitude. She was more optimistic and less prone to stress and anxiety. She even started practising meditation and other mindfulness techniques to help her stay focused on positive thoughts.

It's important to remember that our thoughts have a powerful impact on how we feel. By choosing to think positively, we can break the cycle of negativity and start to feel better. It may not solve our problems completely, but it's a helpful tool for improving our mood and overall well-being. So, the next time we feel frustrated or stressed out, let us try to take a step back and ask ourselves, 'What am I thinking right now?' Then, we need to find a more positive way to frame the situation. With practice, this can become a habit that leads to a happier and healthier life. The blindfold of beliefs and biases can be difficult to remove. It can feel like we are peeling away layers of ourselves and facing uncomfortable truths. However, this process of unravelling is necessary for us to live authentically and see the world for what it is.

> *'The wound is the place where the light enters you'.*
>
> ***– Rumi***

It is through facing our challenges and limitations that we can grow and become more aware.

Let us explore practical tips and exercises for unravelling the blindfold. We will look at how we can identify and question our beliefs, overcome our biases and cultivate a more open and curious mind-set.

One of the first steps in this process is to become aware of our own beliefs and biases. We can do this by asking ourselves questions such as:

- 'What do I believe to be true about myself and the world?'
- 'Where did these beliefs come from?'
- 'Are they based on evidence or personal experience?'
- 'Are they limiting my potential or helping me to grow?'

Once we have identified our beliefs and biases, we can begin to question them. We can ask ourselves:

- 'Is this belief serving me?'
- 'How might my life be different if I held a different belief?'
- 'What evidence do I have to support this belief?'
- 'What evidence contradicts this belief?'

We can also seek out experiences and perspectives that challenge our beliefs. This might involve travelling to new places, reading books that challenge our assumptions, seeking out conversations with people who hold different viewpoints or even seeking the help of a life coach who is experienced and has successfully realized their true self.

Finally, we can cultivate a more open and curious mind-set. This involves approaching life with a sense of wonder and a willingness to learn.

> *'I have no special talent, I am only passionately curious'.*
>
> ***– Albert Einstein***

Through these exercises and practices, we can begin to unravel the blindfold of beliefs and biases and cultivate a more assured and expansive way of living.

> *'Vulnerability is the birthplace of innovation, creativity and change'.* ***– Brené Brown***

Let us embrace our vulnerabilities and unravel the blindfold to discover new possibilities for ourselves and the world.

Note to Self

09

Challenging Your Biases

Many of us hold biases and stereotypes about people from different cultures. One way to challenge these biases is through travel. When we travel to new places and meet people from different backgrounds, we have the opportunity to challenge our assumptions and broaden our perspectives.

Someone who grew up in a predominantly white, middle-class neighbourhood might have assumptions about people from other racial and socioeconomic backgrounds, which could be influenced by the media and the limited interactions they have had in their lives.

But if this person travels to a country where they are in the minority, they might have a very different experience. They might experience discrimination or prejudice themselves, which can help them empathize with others who face similar challenges.

They might also have the opportunity to connect with people from different backgrounds and learn about their experiences. This can help them to break down stereotypes and biases and cultivate a more open and curious mind-set.

Many of us hold limiting beliefs that prevent us from reaching our full potential. These beliefs might be about our abilities, our worthiness or our potential for success.

Cultivating curiosity through learning

Cultivating a more open and curious mind-set can involve a commitment to lifelong learning. When we approach life with a sense of wonder and a willingness to learn, we can discover new possibilities and connect with others in meaningful ways.

Someone who has always been interested in astronomy might read books, watch documentaries and attend lectures to deepen their knowledge of the subject.

Through this learning process, they might discover new connections between astronomy and other fields, such as philosophy or art. They might also connect with other people who share their passion and learn from their experiences.

In this way, cultivating curiosity can help us to break down the blindfold of beliefs and biases and see the world more expansively.

Practice mindfulness

Mindfulness is the practice of being present and fully engaged in the present moment. By practising mindfulness, we can become more aware of our thoughts, emotions and physical sensations and learn to observe them without judgement. This can help us let go of the stories we tell ourselves and see the world as it truly is.

Challenge our beliefs

Take a closer look at the beliefs and assumptions that guide our behaviour. Ask ourselves whether they are based on reality or just myths. Challenge the beliefs that hold us back and replace them with positive affirmations that reflect our true selves.

Connect with our values

Identify our core values and align our actions with them. Living in alignment with our values can bring a sense of purpose and fulfilment to our life.

Embrace vulnerability

Embrace vulnerability and open yourself up to new experiences and connections. Vulnerability can be scary, but it's also a necessary step in removing the blindfold and living authentically.

The three strategies for dealing with myths, beliefs and biases:

1. **The Stop Sign Technique:** When we are caught up in the whirlwind of negative or unhealthy thoughts, it can be difficult to break free from the cycle. One effective strategy is the Stop Sign Technique. This involves imagining a stop sign in our mind's eye and saying 'stop' to ourselves whenever we notice

a negative or unhelpful thought creeping in. This simple but powerful technique can help interrupt the flow of thoughts and give us a moment of space to refocus our attention on more positive or productive thoughts. It is a simple yet effective tool that relies on the creative ability of our minds to develop vivid mental images that serve as a firewall against negative thoughts. With regular practice, this technique can be an essential tool in one's self-care and personal growth journey.

2. **The Power of Written Questions:** Another strategy for dealing with myths, beliefs and biases is to put our thoughts on trial by asking ourselves written questions. This involves writing down a belief or assumption that we are holding and then challenging it with a series of questions. For example, if we are struggling with imposter syndrome at work, we might write down the belief 'I'm not qualified for this job' and then ask ourselves questions like 'What evidence do I have to support this belief?' or 'What are some examples of times when I have succeeded in this job?' This can help us uncover the underlying assumptions and biases that may be holding us back and shift our perspective to a more positive and empowering one.

3. **Mindfulness and Self-reflection:** Finally, a powerful strategy for dealing with myths, beliefs and biases is mindfulness and self-reflection. This involves taking regular moments to tune in to our thoughts and emotions, without judgement or criticism. By

becoming more aware of our inner world, we can start to notice patterns and tendencies that may be shaping our beliefs and behaviours. This can help us identify areas where we may be holding onto limiting or negative beliefs and work to release them. Mindfulness and self-reflection can also help us cultivate a more compassionate and accepting attitude toward ourselves and others, which can lead to greater peace and fulfilment in our life.

The benefits of living a life without the blindfold are many. We will experience greater self-awareness, inner peace and fulfilment. We will also be more open to new experiences and connections, and we will have the courage to pursue our dreams and live our best life.

Here are some examples of individuals who have removed the blindfold and found their true selves:

- **Brené Brown**—she is a research professor and author who has written extensively about vulnerability, shame and authenticity. Her work has inspired millions of people to embrace their vulnerability and live their life to their fullest potential.
- **Oprah Winfrey**—she is a media mogul and philanthropist who has been open about her struggles with self-doubt and self-esteem. Through her work, she has encouraged others to embrace their true selves and live their best lives.
- **Malala Yousafzai**—she is an activist for women's education and the youngest Nobel Prize laureate. Despite facing life-threatening challenges, she has remained true to her beliefs and has inspired millions to stand up for what they believe in.

Remember that removing the blindfold is a journey, not a destination. It requires a commitment to self-awareness, self-love and self-compassion. By taking small steps each day, we can remove the veil and live the life we truly deserve.

By learning to remove our blindfold, we can experience the world with greater clarity and see things as they truly are, without the limitations of our beliefs and biases. As we journey through life, it's easy to get caught up in the busyness and chaos of the world around us. However, by learning to remove our blindfolds, we can start to live with greater intention and purpose. We can make choices that are aligned with our values and beliefs, and experience greater fulfilment and happiness in our lives.

Ultimately, **The Blindfold** is a book about self-discovery and personal growth. It's a call to action for readers to take ownership of their lives and start the journey toward a more assured and fulfilling existence. With its engaging tone, insightful anecdotes and practical strategies, this book is a must-read for anyone who is looking to unlock their full potential and live their best life.

Finding Inner Peace through Self-growth

We all can control and be aware of our thoughts. For those of us who have anxiety issues or are undergoing treatment for depression, it's important to take it slow and not overwhelm ourselves. The aim of the journey of self-growth is ultimately to be kinder to ourselves and to become more mindful of how we process information so that we can shift from unhealthy thinking to healthy thinking.

This does not mean that we should be rude to others and expect the same awareness from them. When we change ourselves and our internal environment, it can have a positive effect on our external environment. People around us may start to take notice and even change their behaviour, and even if they remain passive, we will still be a changed person. We will be thinking differently and no longer holding others responsible for our hurt, nor will we be holding ourselves to blame for anything that does not go our way.

For those who want to get the most out of their journey of self-growth and discovery, I highly recommend seeking out an expert mentor who can guide and support you. There is a wealth of information available online in the form of books, videos and podcasts, but the value of having a mentor is immeasurable. It's like having a dedicated coach helping us to reach our full potential.

At the end of the day, the methods and techniques discussed in the book are like first-aid to help us heal our wounds. Mentors are the ones who will be there to support us and pick us up whenever we stumble.

Note to Self

Blurb

> *'The only thing that matters in life is your own opinion about yourself"'.*
>
> ***– Osho***

The outer world is a reflection of our inner world.

We attract what we are.

We all know this, but we do not make a conscious effort towards implementing it in our lives.

Are you one of those people who feel they are not being valued?

Do you often say 'I am not being loved?'

Do you often get trapped in unhealthy thinking?

In this engaging and thought-provoking self-help guide, we will explore the concept of the blindfold and how it impacts our perceptions, beliefs and decision-making processes. We will learn how common myths and misconceptions can blind us from seeing the truth and also discover strategies for identifying and overcoming them.

The Blindfold offers practical tools and techniques for removing the blindfold and realizing our true selves. Whether we are struggling with negative self-talk, limiting beliefs or unhelpful thought patterns, this book will provide us with the tools we need to break free and live a more genuine and fulfilling life.

With a casual, direct tone and engaging anecdotes and examples, this is the perfect guide for anyone looking to unlock their full potential and live their best life. Whether we are new to personal growth or a self-help enthusiast, **The Blindfold** is a must-read book that will inspire and empower us to take action and start living the life we deserve.

List of Quotes

1. 'You make your life hard by always being in your head. Life is simple, get out of your head and get into the moment'. -Sylvester Mcnutt
2. 'Live Consciously'. - Pritti M Dhanukka
3. 'You must learn a new way to think for a happy life'. - Pritti M Dhanukka
4. 'We have been blindfolded by our own minds. And our perception of the world is what makes us believe that we are helpless. We have been led to believe that we cannot control the direction of our lives; we live with our blindfolds'. -Pritti M Dhanukka
5. 'Your mind-set matters. It affects everything—from the business and investment decisions you make to the way you raise your children, to your stress levels and overall well-being'. -Peter Diamandis
6. 'We can be blind to the obvious, and we can also be blind to our blindness'. -Daniel Kahneman
7. 'The greatest discovery of my generation is that a human being can alter his life by altering his attitude'. - William James

8. ‘Removing the blindfold can be a daunting and uncomfortable process. It might challenge our beliefs and shake the foundations of our identity. But in doing so, we’ll discover a new sense of clarity, purpose and meaning’. -Pritti M Dhanukka

9. ‘It’s time to take off the blindfold and embrace the world for what it is’. -Pritti M Dhanukka

10. ‘The journey starts here. Let’s embark on this adventure together and unlock the full potential of our lives’. -Pritti M Dhanukka

11. ‘We learn our belief system as very little children, and then we move through life creating experiences to match our beliefs. Look back in your own life and notice how often you have gone through the same experience’. -Louise L. Hay

12. ‘Negative thinking patterns can be immensely deceptive and persuasive, and change is rarely easy. But with patience and persistence, I believe that nearly all individuals suffering from depression can improve and experience a sense of joy and self-esteem once again’. - David D. Burns

13. ‘Life has no limitations, except the ones you make’. -Les Brown

14. ‘Our beliefs about what we are and what we can be precisely determine what we can be’. -Tony Robbins

15. ‘Whether you think you can or you think you can’t—you’re right’. -Henry Ford

16. 'The truth will set you free, but first, it will piss you off'. - Gloria Steinem

17. 'The wound is the place where the light enters you'. - Rumi

18. 'I have no special talent, I am only passionately curious'. - Albert Einstein

19. 'Vulnerability is the birthplace of innovation, creativity, and change'. - Brené Brown

20. 'The only thing that matters in life is your own opinion about yourself"'. - Osho

List of some Limiting Beliefs

Here is a list of the most common limiting beliefs that people may hold:

- ☐ 'I'm not good enough'.
- ☐ 'I'm not smart enough'.
- ☐ 'I don't deserve to be successful'.
- ☐ 'I'm not worthy of love'.
- ☐ 'Money is evil'.
- ☐ 'I'm stuck in my circumstances'.
- ☐ 'I don't have enough time'.
- ☐ 'I can't change who I am'.
- ☐ 'Success requires luck or connections'.
- ☐ 'I'm too old/young'.
- ☐ 'I'm not creative'.
- ☐ 'I'm not talented enough'.
- ☐ 'I'm not confident enough'.
- ☐ 'I'm not popular enough'.
- ☐ 'I'm not strong enough'.
- ☐ 'I'm not thin/fit/athletic enough'.

- ☐ 'I'm not spiritual enough'.
- ☐ 'I'm not lucky'.
- ☐ 'I don't have enough resources'.
- ☐ 'I can't trust people'.
- ☐ 'I'm too busy'.
- ☐ 'I'm too old to learn something new'.
- ☐ 'I'm too introverted to be successful'.
- ☐ 'I'm not educated enough'.
- ☐ 'I don't have enough experience'.
- ☐ 'I'm not attractive enough'.
- ☐ 'I'm not good at networking'.
- ☐ 'I'm not lucky in love'.
- ☐ 'I'm not good at public speaking'.
- ☐ 'I'm not good at sales'.

About the Author

Pritti M Dhanukka, a graduate in Psychology, is a passionate advocate of self-mastery and personal growth. She has a wealth of experience in this field, having successfully transformed her own life through years of introspection and practice. Pritti is a certified life coach, cognitive-behavioural life coach and practitioner of neuro-linguistic programming (NLP), with international certifications in each of these areas.

Married to a daunting husband for twenty-four years and the proud mother of three amazing children, Pritti understands the challenges of balancing personal and professional responsibilities. She has also lived in a joint family for twenty-four years, which provided her with valuable insights into the dynamics of family relationships.

Pritti's journey towards self-discovery and resilience began later in life, as she started her career at the age of forty-three. Her transformation inspired her to help others unlock their full potential and achieve success and fulfilment in their lives. Through her programs and services, Pritti provides individuals with practical tools and strategies to develop resilience, emotional intelligence and wisdom.

In her book, **The Blindfol**d, Pritti shares her experiences and insights into the journey toward self-mastery and personal growth. Drawing on her expertise in psychology, life coaching and NLP, she provides actionable content and support to help readers overcome their fears, achieve their goals and create lasting transformations in their lives.

Pritti's commitment to help individuals achieve self-realization and personal development is evident in the practical and accessible approach she takes in her book.

Whether you are a young adult stepping into the real world to start your journey of life, a professional looking to advance your career, an entrepreneur seeking to grow your business or simply someone who wants to live life to the fullest: Pritti's book offers valuable insights and tools to support you on your journey towards self-discovery and transformation.

CONDUCTING WORKSHOPS
AND
SPEAKING ENGAGEMENTS
Lifecoach@lifecoachpritti.com

www.ingramcontent.com/pod-product-compliance
Lightning Source LLC
LaVergne TN
LVHW050319160826
845677LV00014B/3474
* 9 7 9 8 8 8 9 8 6 9 9 8 6 *